Four Kinds of Sentences

Name _____

Rule   Always begin a sentence with a capital letter. End a **statement** or a **command** with a period. End a **question** with a question mark. End an **exclamation** with an exclamation point.

Example

Grizzly bears are fascinating creatures. (**statement**)
Do they live in all parts of the world? (**question**)
Grizzly bears are huge! (**exclamation**)
Tell me more about bears. (**command**)

Exercise   Rewrite each sentence using the correct capitalization and punctuation.

1. grizzly bears live in Wyoming, Montana, Idaho, Alaska, and western Canada _____

    _____

2. some grizzlies are eight feet in length _____

    _____

3. did you know that male grizzlies can weigh 800 pounds _____

    _____

4. these bears are huge _____

5. they can run very quickly _____

6. that's incredible speed _____

7. what do grizzly bears eat _____

8. they eat acorns, roots, berries, and leaves _____

    _____

9. they also eat fish, birds, insects, and small mammals _____

    _____

10. grizzlies love honey, too _____

11. help me find out more about grizzly bears _____

    _____

Statements

Name _____

Rule A **statement** is a sentence that tells something. It begins with a capital letter and ends with a period.

Example

Mercury is the planet closest to the sun.

Exercise If the sentence is a statement put an **S** on the line and add a period. If the sentence is not, put an **X** on the line.

_____ 1. Mercury revolves around the sun once every 88 earth-days

_____ 2. Mercury travels around the sun at 30 miles per second

_____ 3. Its days are as long as about 180 earth-days

_____ 4. That is because Mercury rotates so slowly as it revolves around the sun

_____ 5. Can you see Mercury without a telescope

_____ 6. Because of its nearness to the bright sun, it is hard to see

_____ 7. Mercury is two-fifths the size of the earth

_____ 8. Mercury's surface seems to be much like our moon's

_____ 9. The planet has flat plains, steep cliffs, and many craters

_____ 10. Would Mercury be too hot for life as we know it

• Write two statements telling why you would or would not want to visit Mercury.

_____

_____

_____

_____

Questions

Rule A **question** is a sentence that asks something. It begins with a capital letter and ends with a question mark.

Example

Why is Mars known as the red planet?

Exercise If the sentence is a question, add a question mark and color the circle **red**. If it is not a question, put an **X** on the circle.

○ 1. How many miles is Mars from the sun

○ 2. Can you see Mars without a telescope

○ 3. Mars is the fourth planet from the sun

○ 4. Did you know there are only two planets which are smaller than Mars

○ 5. Would plants and animals be able to live on Mars

○ 6. What is the surface temperature on Mars

○ 7. Does Mars have polar caps like the earth

○ 8. Are there mountains and volcanoes on the planet

○ 9. Is much of its surface desertlike

○ 10. When do you think a manned spacecraft will go to Mars

• Rewrite each statement as a question by changing the word order.

1. Clouds can be seen on Mars.

_____

2. Mars does have two moons.

_____

3. The moons are named Phobos and Deimos.

_____

4. Space probes have landed on Mars.

_____

Exclamatory and Command Sentences

Name _____

Rule An **exclamatory sentence** is a sentence that shows strong feeling or surprise. It begins with a capital letter and ends with an exclamation point.

Example

I won a trip around the world!

Rule A **command sentence** tells someone to do something. A command begins with a capital letter and ends with a period.

Example

Get my suitcase.

Exercise Add the correct punctuation to the end of each sentence. Then color the exclamatory sentences **blue** and the commands **green**.

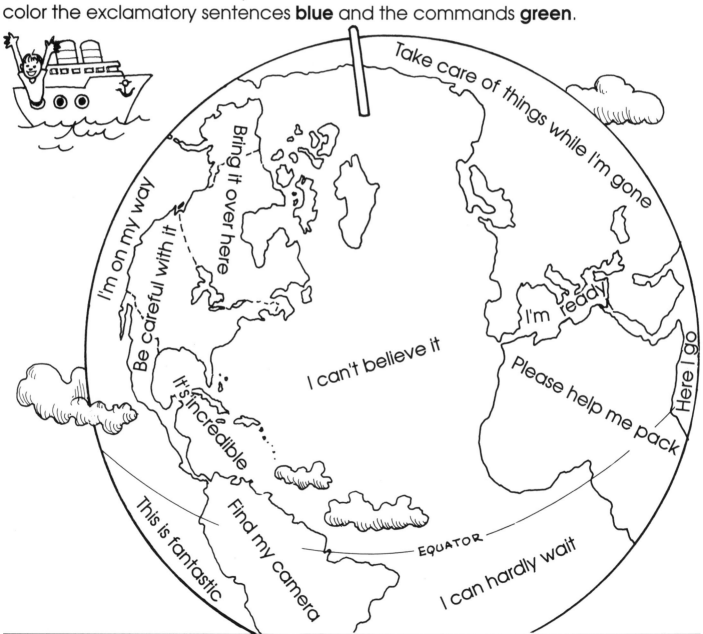

I'm on my way

Be careful with it

Bring it over here

Take care of things while I'm gone

I'm ready

I can't believe it

It's incredible

Please help me pack

Here I go

This is fantastic

Find my camera

EQUATOR

I can hardly wait

Word Order in Sentences

Name _____

Rule You can often make a question out of a statement by changing the word order of the sentence.

Example

My family is going on a camping trip. (**statement**)

Is my family going on a camping trip? (**question**)

Exercise Change the word order to make each statement a question and each question a statement. Write the new sentence on the line.

1. Mom and Dad are going to take turns driving.

_____

2. Ellen is getting the gear together.

_____

3. James is packing the car trunk.

_____

4. Will it be dark when we arrive at the lake?

_____

5. Joey's job is to put up the tent.

_____

6. I can help by inflating the air mattresses.

_____

7. Will we sit around the fire and tell stories?

_____

8. Will I be allowed to roast marshmallows the first night?

_____

9. Camping is fun for most families.

_____

Nouns

Name _____

Rule A **noun** names a person, place, or thing.

Example

A **teacher** at my **school** read a **book**.

Exercise Color each book blue if the word in it is a noun. Put an **X** on each word which is not a noun.

banker

lifeguard

castle

home

beautiful

happy

mall

lumber

breeze

druggist

firefighter

daisy

city

every

ballerina

aunt

More Nouns

Rule A **noun** names a person, place, or thing.

Example

*Some **scientists** study **plants** and **animals** that live in tropical **forests**.*

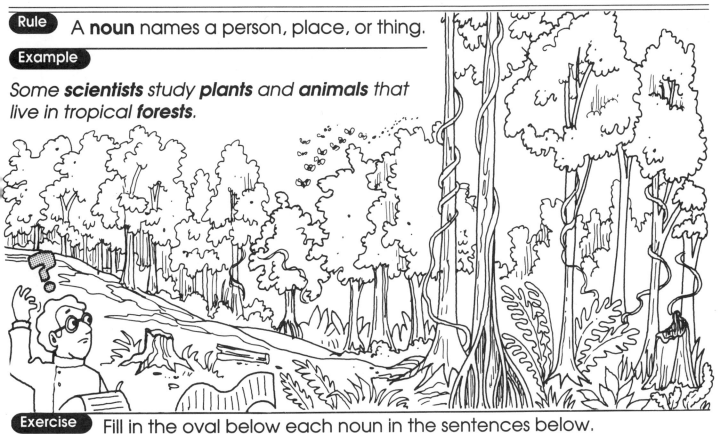

Exercise Fill in the oval below each noun in the sentences below.

1. A study is being done on treetops.

2. This part of the forest is called the canopy.

3. A scientist rides to the top of the trees.

4. A construction crane lifts a cage above the forest.

5. Then the scientist can see and record information.

6. This kind of work can be dangerous.

7. Killer bees live in the treetops.

8. The scientist could use a fire extinguisher if the bees attack.

9. The cold gas of the extinguisher would make the bees inactive.

10. Scientists want to study how plants and animals live in the canopy.

Singular and Plural Nouns

Name _____

Rule A **singular noun** names one person, place, or thing.

Example

*The **girl** built a **birdfeeder** in her **backyard**.*

Rule A **plural noun** names more than one person, place, or thing.

Example

*The **girls** built **birdfeeders** in their **backyards**.*

Exercise Underline the singular nouns with one line and the plural nouns with two lines.

1. One girl saw three cardinals land at her feeder.

2. The bluejays cracked seeds on the side of the feeder with their bills.

3. A squirrel chased off some little sparrows.

4. As the children watched, some Canada geese flew overhead.

5. Pictures in books helped the children identify many birds.

• Write a sentence for each of these singular or plural nouns.

(berries) _____

(city) _____

(trees) _____

(men) _____

(woman) _____

(wrens) _____

Plural Nouns

Rule A **plural noun** names more than one person, place, or thing. Add **-s** to make most nouns plural.

Example

boys, parks, baseballs

Rule If the singular noun ends in **sh, ch, x, s,** or **ss,** add **-es** to form the plural.

Example

wishes, lunches, boxes, gases, glasses

Exercise Make each noun in parentheses plural by adding **-s** or **-es**. Write the plural nouns in the blanks.

All the _____ and _____ sat on _____
            (mother)   (father)   (bench)

to watch the _____ . The _____ ran onto the
              (game)   (team)

field amidst the _____ of the crowd. In the first game Dave
                  (cheer)

got two _____ and no _____ . Suzie made
          (hit)   (strike)

three fine _____ for her _____ . The
            (catch)   (teammate)

two _____ were proud of the _____ .
      (coach)   (kid)

• Write the plural of each word.

1. kiss _____   6. fox _____

2. window _____   7. watch _____

3. ax _____   8. flash _____

4. bunch _____   9. wagon _____

5. pencil _____   10. dress _____

More Plural Nouns

Name _____

Follow these rules to form some **plural nouns**.

- If the singular noun ends in a vowel and a **y**, add -**s**.
    day, days
    toy, toys

- If the singular noun ends in a consonant and a **y**, change the **y** to **i** and add -**es**.
    fly, flies
    candy, candies

- Usually, if the singular noun ends in **f** or **fe**, change the **f** or **fe** to **v** and add -**es**.
    thief, thieves
    life, lives

Exercise Write the plural form of each noun.

1. baby _____

2. turkey _____

3. knife _____

4. sky _____

5. pansy _____

6. guppy _____

7. elf _____

8. wife _____

9. try _____

10. key _____

11. boy _____

12. shelf _____

13. lady _____

14. chimney _____

15. hoof _____

16. gypsy _____

17. monkey _____

18. cooky _____

19. pony _____

20. hobby _____

Proper Nouns

Rule A **proper noun** names a specific person, place, or thing. A proper noun is always capitalized.

Example

John came to *St. Louis* to visit the *Gateway Arch*.

Exercise Circle the proper nouns in each sentence.

1. The students in Mr. Hoover's class at Buder School had visited many places during their summer vacation.

2. In June, Robbie visited his sister Kate in Georgia.

3. When he was in Atlanta he saw a baseball game at Fulton County Stadium.

4. Marco had fun at Disney World in Orlando, Florida.

5. His family also went to the Kennedy Space Center.

6. Carla enjoyed a ride on the Powell Street cable car in San Francisco.

7. Then she took a boat ride to Alcatraz and saw the Golden Gate Bridge.

8. Last Thursday Carmen brought her pictures of the Grand Canyon to show us.

9. She thought it was better than seeing the Royal Gorge in Colorado.

10. Sabrina said she will fly to Hawaii for her vacation next July.

Possessive Nouns

Name _____

Rule and Example A **possessive noun** shows ownership or possession.

- Add an **apostrophe** and an **s** (**'s**) to a singular noun.

    *the dog**'s** bone, Chris**'s** puppy*

- Add an **apostrophe** and an **s** (**'s**) to a plural noun that does not end in **s**.

    *the children**'s** turtle*

- Add an **apostrophe** (**'**) to a plural noun that ends in **s**.

    *the two pets**'** cages*

Exercise Read the sentences. Circle the answers.

1. Our class's pet show was last Friday.
   How many classes had a pet show?   one   more than one

2. The students' pets were interesting.
   How many students had pets?   one   more than one

3. The girl's hamster got out of the cage.
   How many girls had hamsters?   one   more than one

4. The snake's meal was a mouse.
   How many snakes were there?   one   more than one

5. The mice's cage was next to the snakes.
   How many mice were there?   one   more than one

6. The puppies' barking was disturbing.
   How many puppies were there?   one   more than one

7. The chicken's clucking was noisy.
   How many chickens were there?   one   more than one

8. The box turtle's shell protected it well.
   How many box turtles were there?   one   more than one

Action Verbs

Rule An **action verb** is a verb that shows action.

Example

*My family **drove** to Arizona last summer.*

Exercise Color the space green if the word is an action verb. Color the space tan if it is not.

Present Tense Verbs

Name _____

Example

*The track meet **begins** at 3 o'clock.*

*The students **want** our school to win.*

Exercise Circle the present tense form of the verb. Write it in the blank.

1. Carl _____ out of the starting block.
   (sprang, springs)

2. Samantha _____ the fastest of all.
   (ran, runs)

3. Pete _____ the javelin a long distance.
   (threw, throws)

4. In the long jump, Mandy _____ over four feet.
   (jumped, jumps)

5. Daniel _____ faster than anyone.
   (sprinted, sprints)

6. The two boys _____ over the hurdles.
   (leap, lept)

7. Dave _____ the discus farther than Aaron.
   (hurled, hurls)

8. Tommy _____ in the last lap of his race.
   (fell, falls)

9. The girls _____ to race.
   (start, started)

10. Our team _____ the track meet.
    (won, wins)

• On a separate paper, write five sentences using these present tense verbs correctly: hops, shows, gives, take, smiles.

Past Tense Verbs

Name _____

Rule and Example **Past tense verbs** show action that has already happened.

Rule 1: Add -**ed** to most verbs to show the past tense. If the verb already ends in **e**, drop the **e** and add -**ed**.

*walk**ed**, smil**ed***

Rule 2: If a one-syllable verb ends with a consonant preceded by a vowel, double the final consonant before adding -**ed**.

*plan**ned**, drop**ped***

Rule 3: If the verb ends with a **y** preceded by a consonant, change the **y** to **i** and add -**ed**.

*carr**ied**, fr**ied***

Exercise Write the past tense of these verbs on the blanks. Then color the picture, using the code to show how to make the past tense of each verb.

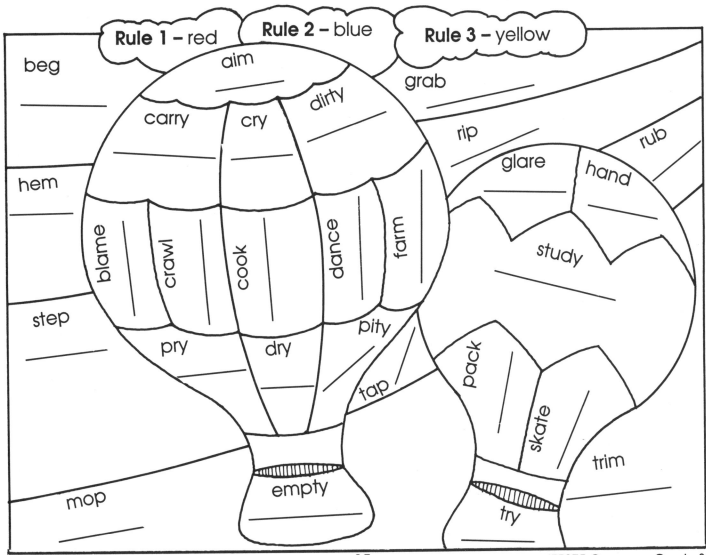

Rule 1 – red   Rule 2 – blue   Rule 3 – yellow

beg, aim, grab, carry, cry, dirty, rip, rub, glare, hand, hem, blame, crawl, cook, dance, farm, study, step, pry, dry, pity, pack, tap, skate, trim, mop, empty, try

Helping Verbs

Name _____

Rule A **verb phrase** contains a **main verb** and a **helping verb**. The helping verb usually comes in front of the main verb. **Has** and **have** can be used as helping verbs.

Example

*We **have learned** about dental health.*

  ↑   ↑

helping   main
verb   verb

Exercise Underline the helping verb and circle the main verb in each sentence.

1. A dental hygienist has come to talk to our class.

2. We have written questions ahead of time to ask her.

3. I have wondered if it is really necessary to brush after every meal.

4. We have waited to be shown the proper way to floss our teeth.

5. We have learned the names of all the different kinds of teeth.

6. We have listed incisors, cuspids, and molars as names of teeth.

7. Most of us have known the parts of a tooth for a long time.

8. The teacher has given us a list of snack foods that may cause cavities.

9. Nearly half the class has eaten too much sugar today.

10. I have experimented with different kinds of toothpaste to see which ones cleaned teeth best.

• Write six sentences using a different verb phrase in each.

_____

_____

_____

_____

_____

Linking Verbs

Name _____

Rule A **linking verb** does not show action. Instead, it links the subject of the sentence with
a noun or adjective in the predicate. **Am, is,
are, was,** and **were** are linking verbs.

Example

*Thomas Jefferson **was** President of the
United States.*

Exercise   Write a linking verb in each blank.

1. The class's writing assignment _____ a report on U.S. Presidents.

2. The reports _____ due tomorrow.

3. I _____ glad I chose to write about Thomas Jefferson, the third
   President of our country.

4. Early in his life, he _____ the youngest delegate to the First
   Continental Congress.

5. The colonies _____ angry at England.

6. Thomas Jefferson _____ a great writer, so he was asked to
   help write the Declaration of Independence.

7. The signing of that document _____ an historical event.

8. Later, as President, Jefferson _____ responsible for the
   Louisiana Purchase.

9. He _____ the first President to live in the White House.

10. Americans _____ fortunate today for the part played in our
    country's history by Thomas Jefferson.

©1994 Instructional Fair, Inc.   17   IF5075 Grammar Grade 3

Future Tense Verbs

Name _____

Rule **Future tense verbs** show action that will happen in the future. Use the **helping verb** *will* with a **main verb** to form the future tense.

Example

*An astronaut **will wear** a special suit tomorrow.*
        ↑   ↑
   helping   main
   verb   verb

Exercise In each blank, write the future tense of the verb in parentheses.

1. The seven astronauts _____ for a year before going on the next trip.
   (practice)

2. NASA _____ a space shuttle on Wednesday
   (launch)
   from the John F. Kennedy Space Center.

3. The spacecraft _____ Earth 127 times.
   (orbit)

4. The mission _____ ten days.
   (last)

5. The shuttle _____ 3.3 million miles.
   (travel)

6. One astronaut _____ the mechanical arm
   (operate)
   during the night.

7. One experiment _____ the effects of
   (demonstrate)
   weightlessness on insects.

8. I _____ the crew at work on television.
   (watch)

9. One astronaut _____ a walk in space
   (take)
   tomorrow.

10. The shuttle _____ at Edwards Air Force Base.
    (land)

Irregular Verbs

Name _____

Example

Present	Past	Past with Helpers
ring	rang	(has, have) rung
see	saw	(has, have) seen

Exercise Fill in the missing verbs in the chart.

Present	Past	Past with Helpers
do, does		(has, have) done
go, goes	went	(has, have)
know, knows		(has, have) known
fall, falls		(has, have) fallen
stand, stands		(has, have) stood
speak, speaks	spoke	(has, have)
write, writes		(has, have) written
draw, draws	drew	(has, have)
bring, brings	brought	(has, have)
teach, teaches		(has, have) taught

• Circle the correct verb in the parentheses.

1. Dad and I (went, gone) on a walk in the woods one morning.

2. More than six inches of snow has (fall, fallen).

3. The tall trees (stands, stood) silently in their overcoats of white.

4. A snowshoe rabbit (ran, run) away as we approached it.

5. We (heard, hears) a bluejay's shrill call from the oak tree.

6. A chipmunk was (saw, seen) on an old stump, warming itself in the sunlight.

7. An owl (kept, keep) watch from its perch overhead.

8. It has (took, taken) us nearly an hour to circle back home.

9. Mom (make, made) hot cocoa to warm us after our walk.

10. Dad and I (drank, drinks) it in front of the fire.

More Irregular Verbs

Rule Past tense verbs that are not formed by adding **-ed** are called **irregular verbs**.

Example

Present	**Past**
sing	sang

Exercise Circle the present tense verb in each pair of irregular verbs.

1. won	win	4. tell	told	7. say	said
2. feel	felt	5. eat	ate	8. came	come
3. built	build	6. blew	blow	9. grew	grow

• Write the past tense of each irregular verb.

1. throw _____ 4. sing _____ 7. swim _____

2. wear _____   5. lose _____ 8. sit _____

3. hold _____   6. fly _____   9. sell _____

• In each blank, write the past tense of each irregular verb in parentheses.

1. I _____ my library book to my sister. (give)

2. She _____ for school before I did. (leave)

3. She _____ the bus at the corner. (catch)

4. My sister _____ my book on the way to school. (lose)

5. My sister _____ back to find it. (go)

Subjects of Sentences

Name _____

Rule The **subject** of a sentence tells **whom** or **what** the sentence is about.

Example

The buffalo provided the Plains Indians with many things.

↑
(subject)

Exercise Underline the subject of each sentence.

1. The Plains Indians used almost every part of the buffalo.

2. Their tepees were made of buffalo hides.

3. Clothing was made from the hides of buffalo and deer.

4. Plains Indians ate the meat of the buffalo.

5. Buffalo stomachs were used as pots for cooking.

6. Bones were used for tools and utensils.

7. The tail was used as a fly swatter.

8. Horns were used as scrapers and cups.

9. The buffalo manure was dried and used for fuel.

10. A kind of glue could be made from the hooves.

• If the word group could be the subject of a sentence, put a check mark (✔) on the line. If it could not be the subject of a sentence, put an **X**.

____ 1. feathers, beads, and paint   ____ 4. wore moccasins

____ 2. the headdress   ____ 5. bear claw necklaces

____ 3. decorated their clothes   ____ 6. the chief

Simple and Complete Subjects

Name _____

Rule The **complete subject** contains all the words in the subject part of the sentence. The **simple subject** is the main word in the complete subject.

Example

(simple subject)
↓
Some animals *may become endangered during your lifetime.*
↑
(complete subject)

Exercise Underline the complete subject. Then circle its simple subject.

1. The Pacific coastal waters are home to the sea otters.

2. Herds of sea otters live near the shores of North America and Siberia.

3. These creatures of the sea seldom leave the water.

4. Their thick fur protects them from the cold water.

5. Man-made disasters are responsible for harming the sea otters.

6. Huge oil spills may cause the death of sea otters.

7. A sea otter's fur can become soaked with oil.

8. Then its coat cannot keep it warm.

9. The unfortunate result is that the otter may die.

10. The shellfish which otters eat are also threatened by oil spills.

• Write a complete subject for each simple subject.

1. seals _____

2. island _____

3. whales _____

4. laws _____

Compound Subjects

Rule A **compound subject** has two or more simple subjects joined with the word *and*.

Example

Toads *are amphibians.* ***Frogs*** *are amphibians.*

Toads and frogs *are amphibians.*

Exercise If the sentence has a compound subject, write **CS** in the blank. If the sentence does not have a compound subject, write **NO**.

_____ 1. Most amphibians spend part of their life as a water animal and part as a land animal.

_____ 2. Frogs and salamanders are amphibians.

_____ 3. A salamander has a long body and a tail.

_____ 4. Adult frogs and toads do not have tails.

_____ 5. This makes it easier for them to move on the land.

_____ 6. Frogs use their strong hind legs for leaping.

_____ 7. The eyes and nostrils of a frog are on top of its head.

_____ 8. Tree frogs are expert jumpers and can cling to things.

_____ 9. Horned toads are not amphibians.

_____ 10. They are really reptiles.

• Combine the subject parts of the two sentences to make a compound subject. Write the new sentence on the line.

1. Toads return to the water to lay eggs. Frogs return to the water to lay eggs.

_____

2. Newts have tails. Salamanders have tails.

_____

3. Tree frogs are noisy. Bullfrogs are noisy.

_____

Predicates of Sentences

Name _____

Rule The **predicate** of a sentence tells what the subject of the sentence is or does.

Example

Juan *is interested in collecting rocks*.

↑   ↑
(subject)   (predicate)

Exercise Underline the predicate part of each sentence with two lines.

1. Juan looks for rocks everywhere he goes.

2. He has found many interesting rocks in his own backyard.

3. Juan showed me a piece of limestone with fossils in it.

4. Limestone is a kind of sedimentary rock.

5. It is formed underwater from the shells of animals.

6. Juan told me that some rocks come from deep inside the earth.

7. Molten rock comes out of a volcano.

8. The lava cools to form igneous rock.

9. Heat and pressure inside the earth cause igneous and sedimentary rock to change form.

10. This changed rock is called metamorphic rock.

11. Metamorphic rock is often used in building.

12. I want to become a rock hound, too!

• Write a predicate for each sentence.

1. Rock collecting _____

2. Some rocks _____

3. Sandstone _____

4. Rocks and minerals _____

Simple and Complete Predicates

Name _____

Rule   The **complete predicate** contains all of the words in the predicate part of the sentence.

The **simple predicate** is the verb in the complete predicate.

Example

simple predicate
↓
Arthur Ashe **was** a great American tennis player.
                    ↑
           complete predicate

Exercise   Underline the complete predicate with two lines. Circle the simple predicate.

1. Arthur lived in Richmond, Virginia, as a boy.

2. He played tennis in a neighborhood park.

3. Arthur moved to St. Louis, Missouri, to improve his tennis game.

4. He went to college at UCLA on a tennis scholarship.

5. He captured the intercollegiate singles and doubles titles.

6. Arthur Ashe was the first African American winner of a major men's singles championship.

7. Arthur won the U.S. (amateur) singles and open singles championships.

8. Arthur became the number one tennis player in the world in 1975.

9. Mr. Ashe represented the United States for ten years as a member of the U.S. Davis Cup team.

10. Arthur Ashe served as a role model for young African American athletes.

Compound Predicates

Rule   A **compound predicate** has two or more simple predicates joined with the word *and*.

Example

*Dad **picks up** Sam. Dad **drives** Sam to the dentist.*

*Dad **picks up and drives** Sam to the dentist.*

Exercise   If the sentence has a compound predicate, write **CP** on the line. If it does not have a compound predicate, write **NO**.

_____ 1. Dad and Sam park the car and go inside.

_____ 2. Sam reads and watches TV while waiting for the dentist.

_____ 3. Dad visits with another patient.

_____ 4. The hygienist comes into the room and gets Sam.

_____ 5. The hygienist cleans, polishes, and X-rays Sam's teeth.

_____ 6. The dentist examines Sam's teeth and checks the X-rays.

_____ 7. The dentist gives Sam a toothbrush to take home.

_____ 8. Sam thanks the dentist.

_____ 9. Dad pays the dentist.

_____ 10. Sam promises to brush his teeth daily.

• Combine the predicate parts of the two sentences to make a compound predicate. Write the new sentence on the line.

1. Sam wiggles his loose tooth. Sam pulls his loose tooth.

   _____

2. Sam smiles. Sam shows Dad the empty space in his mouth.

   _____

3. Dad laughs. Dad hugs Sam.

   _____

Compound Sentences

Name _____

Rule Use a comma and the word **and** to connect two simple sentences to make a **compound sentence**.

Example

George Washington was born in 1732 **, and** *Abraham Lincoln was born in 1809.*

Exercise Combine the two sentences to make a compound sentence.

1. George was raised in Virginia. Abe grew up in Kentucky.

   _____

2. George Washington was a surveyor. Abraham Lincoln was a lawyer.

   _____

3. Washington was commander in chief in the Revolutionary War. Lincoln was the U.S. President during the Civil War.

   _____

   _____

• Write the two simple sentences that make up each compound sentence.

1. George Washington is my favorite president, and Abraham Lincoln is your favorite.

   _____

   _____

2. Washington was our first president, and Lincoln was the sixteenth.

   _____

   _____

3. The Washington Monument is in Washington, D.C., and the Lincoln Memorial is there, also.

   _____

   _____

Subject-Verb Agreement

Name _____

Rule The subject and verb in a sentence must agree in number.

Example

An adult **plant makes** *seeds.*
↑ ↑
singular singular
noun verb

Adult **plants make** *seeds.*
↑ ↑
plural plural
noun verb

Exercise If the subject and verb agree, circle the letter under **Yes** at the end of the sentence. If they do not, circle the letter under **No**.

	Yes	No
1. Seeds travel in many ways.	A	R
2. Sometimes seeds falls in the water.	T	D
3. Then they may floats a long distance.	S	L
4. Animals gather seeds in the fall.	O	E
5. Squirrels digs holes to bury their seeds.	M	A
6. Cardinals likes to eat sunflower seeds.	J	N
7. The wind scatters seeds, too.	E	G
8. Dogs carries seeds that are stuck in their fur.	L	N
9. Some seeds stick to people's clothing.	I	T
10. People plants seeds to grow baby plants.	R	D

• Write the circled letters on the lines above the matching numerals to spell the answer to this question: **Which lion scatters seeds?**

___   ___ ___ ___ ___ ___ ___ ___ ___ ___
1   10   5   8   2   7   3   9   4   6

IF5075 Grammar Grade 3

Possessive Pronouns

Name _____

Rule A **possessive pronoun** tells who or what owns or possesses something. It can replace a possessive noun or noun phrase. Possessive pronouns can be used before a noun or alone. Used before a noun: *my, your, its, her, his, our,* and *their.* Used alone: *mine, yours, his, hers, ours, yours,* and *theirs.*

Example

That is <u>Jim's</u> book about dinosaurs.   That book about dinosaurs is <u>Jim's</u>.
This is **his** book about dinosaurs.   That book about dinosaurs is **his**.

Exercise Read each pair of sentences. If the correct possessive pronoun is used in the second sentence, circle the letter under **Right**. If it is not, circle the letter under **Wrong**.

		Right	Wrong
1. A paleontologist studies dinosaurs' remains. A paleontologist studies **their** remains.		1. E	L
2. The important discovery was the scientist's. The important discovery was **hers**.		2. R	S
3. She found part of a dinosaur's tooth. She found part of **their** tooth.		3. O	C
4. The tyrannosaurus's weight was seven tons! **Its** weight was seven tons!		4. E	D
5. The reptile's legs were like tree trunks. **Our** legs were like tree trunks.		5. M	O
6. Experts say the tyrannosaurus's short forearms were probably almost useless. Experts say **their** short forearms were probably almost useless.		6. B	U
7. A tyrannosaurus's meal might have been a triceratops. Our meal might have been a triceratops.		7. S	T
8. One theory about the dinosaurs' death is in the book. One theory about **its** death is in the book.		8. K	A
9. The scientist's theory is that a huge meteorite hit the earth. **Their** theory is that a huge meteorite hit the earth.		9. B	S

The tyrannosaurus lived during the _____ _____ _____ _____ _____ _____ _____ _____ _____ _____ Period.
                                       3   2   4   7   8   3   1   5   6   9

Subject Pronouns

Name _____

Rule A **subject pronoun** is a pronoun that is used as the subject of a sentence. *I, you, he, she, it, we,* and *they* are subject pronouns.

Example

Tall tales are fun to read.
They are fun to read.

Exercise Rewrite each sentence. Use the correct subject pronoun to replace the boldfaced words.

1. **One tall tale** is about Pecos Bill.

   _____

2. According to the legend, **Pecos Bill** was born in eastern Texas long ago.

   _____

3. One day **Bill** fell into the Pecos River and almost drowned.

   _____

4. **A mother coyote** pulled him from the water.

   _____

5. **The coyotes** raised Bill as a member of the pack.

   _____

6. One day **a cowboy named Chuck** found Pecos Bill.

   _____

7. **Chuck** told Bill that he was a Texan, not a coyote.

   _____

8. **Bill** decided to become a cowboy, too.

   _____

9. Once **a giant rattlesnake** attacked Bill.

   _____

10. **Bill** squeezed the poison out of the snake.

    _____

Object Pronouns

Name _____

Rule **Object pronouns** are pronouns which come after action verbs in a sentence. *Me, you, him, her, it, us,* and *them* are object pronouns.

Example

Pecos Bill wrestled <u>a gigantic monster.</u>
*Pecos Bill wrestled **it**.*

Exercise Rewrite each sentence. Replace the words in boldfaced type with the correct object pronoun.

1. Pecos Bill invented **cattle roping and branding**.

   _____

2. He scared **a steer** out of its skin with a coyote howl.

   _____

3. Bill used **the hide** to make lassos for all the cowboys.

   _____

4. Bill wanted **a horse** to ride on a roundup.

   _____

5. Bill captured **a wild stallion called Lightning**.

   _____

6. The horse crossed **three states** trying to buck Bill.

   _____

7. Bill calmed **the horse** by singing in coyote language.

   _____

8. Then Bill met **Slewfoot Sue** and fell in love.

   _____

9. Unfortunately, Lightning bucked **Slewfoot Sue** up to the moon.

   _____

10. Bill lassoed **a tornado** to help him save Sue.

   _____

Adjectives

Rule An **adjective** is a word that describes a noun or pronoun. Adjectives answer the questions **how many, what kind,** or **which one**.

Example

Two *students brought **colorful** insects to class.*
　↑　　　　　　　　　　　　　　↑
(how many)　　　　　　　　(what kind)

Exercise Circle the adjective that describes the underlined words.

1. Many <u>scorpions</u> live in the desert.

2. Scorpions have a poisonous <u>sting</u>.

3. A sting can kill a small <u>child</u>.

4. Scorpions hide in dark <u>places</u> during the day.

5. They crawl under rotten <u>logs</u> and beneath rocks.

6. Giant <u>scorpions</u> can be five inches long.

7. Scorpions eat desert <u>insects</u>.

8. They can go without water for one <u>year</u>.

9. Rattlesnakes also live on the southwestern <u>deserts</u>.

10. They are poisonous <u>snakes</u>.

11. The poison comes out of two <u>fangs</u>.

12. The small <u>horned rattler</u> is also called a sidewinder.

13. Rattlesnakes eat small <u>mammals and birds</u>.

Adding Adjectives

Name _____

Rule Using **adjectives** to describe nouns makes writing more interesting and specific.

Example

The **old** woman saw a **spotted** dog in the **busy** street.

Exercise Write an adjective to describe each noun on the line in front of it. Then write a sentence using all three descriptive phrases on the line.

1. _____ janitor _____ floor _____ school

_____

2. _____ clown _____ car _____ circus

_____

3. _____ ranger _____ horse _____ park

_____

4. _____ acrobat _____ rings _____ gym

_____

5. _____ actor _____ play _____ stage

_____

Rule Use a **comma** to separate adjectives in a series.

Example

The **rich, thick** syrup covered the pancakes.

Exercise Write two adjectives to describe each noun. Use a comma to separate the adjectives.

1. _____ cookies   5. _____ apples

2. _____ banana   6. _____ pizza

3. _____ soup   7. _____ hamburger

4. _____ pickles   8. _____ carrots

Adjectives That Compare

Name _____

Add **-er** to most **adjectives** when comparing
two nouns. Add **-est** to most adjectives when
comparing three or more nouns.

Example

*The forecaster said this winter is **colder**
than last winter.*

*It is the **coldest** winter on record.*

Exercise Write the correct form of the adjective in parentheses.

1. The weather map showed that the _____ place of all was
   Fargo, North Dakota. (cold)

2. The _____ city of all was Needles, California. (warm)

3. Does San Diego get _____ than San Francisco? (hot)

4. The _____ snow of all fell in Buffalo, New York. (deep)

5. That snowfall was two inches _____ than in Syracuse. (deep)

6. The _____ place of all was Wichita, Kansas. (windy)

7. The _____ winds of all blew there. (strong)

8. The _____ city in the U.S. was Chicago. (foggy)

9. Seattle was the _____ of all the cities listed on the map. (rainy)

10. It is usually _____ in Seattle than in Portland. (rainy)

11. I just hope tomorrow is _____ than it was today. (sunny)

12. Today has been the _____ day all week. (cloudy)

Proper Adjectives

Rule A **proper adjective** is a word that describes a noun or a pronoun. A proper adjective always begins with a capital letter.

Example

The **American** flag waves proudly over the **United States** capitol.

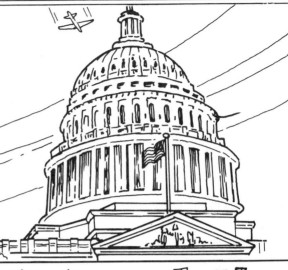

Exercise Underline the proper adjective in each sentence.

1. Spanish music is beautiful.

2. Some Americans buy Japanese cars.

3. I saw the Canadian flag flying.

4. Have you ever eaten Irish stew?

5. The Russian language is hard to learn.

6. Did you say you like French fries?

7. My favorite dog is a German shepherd.

8. The Indian tepee is made of buffalo hides.

9. Do you know how to play Chinese checkers?

10. Dad fished for Alaskan salmon.

• Rewrite each phrase changing the proper noun into a proper adjective.

1. the mountains of Colorado _____

2. skyline of Chicago _____

3. the coast of Florida _____

4. horse from Arabia _____

5. sugarcane of Hawaii _____

Articles

Name _____

Rule and Example **A, an,** and **the** are special adjectives called **articles**.
- Use **a** before singular nouns beginning with a consonant sound.
    a turtle
- Use **an** before singular nouns beginning with a vowel sound or a silent **h**.
    an elephant
- **The** may be used before singular or plural nouns.
    the parrot   *the alligators*

Exercise Circle the article which could be used before each noun.
Hint: Sometimes there is more than one answer.

1. camels	a	an	the	16. octopus	a	an	the
2. cheetah	a	an	the	17. chimpanzee	a	an	the
3. gorillas	a	an	the	18. sharks	a	an	the
4. aardvark	a	an	the	19. opossum	a	an	the
5. eagle	a	an	the	20. lion	a	an	the
6. jaguars	a	an	the	21. pig	a	an	the
7. baboon	a	an	the	22. owl	a	an	the
8. egret	a	an	the	23. dog	a	an	the
9. ibex	a	an	the	24. pony	a	an	the
10. kangaroos	a	an	the	25. whales	a	an	the
11. bird	a	an	the	26. dolphin	a	an	the
12. tigers	a	an	the	27. ostrich	a	an	the
13. ocelot	a	an	the	28. rhinoceros	a	an	the
14. buffalo	a	an	the	29. ox	a	an	the
15. hyenas	a	an	the	30. otter	a	an	the

Adverbs

Rule An **adverb** is a word that can describe a verb. It tells **how, when,** or **where** an action takes place.

Example

*The snow fell **quietly**.* (how)
*It snowed **yesterday**.* (when)
*It fell **everywhere**.* (where)

Exercise Circle the adverbs in the story. Then write them under the correct category in the chart.

The snow began early in the day. Huge snowflakes floated gracefully to the ground. Soon the ground was covered with a blanket of white. Later the wind began to blow briskly. Outside the snow drifted into huge mounds. Now the snow stopped. The children went outdoors. Then they played in the snow there. They went sledding nearby. Others happily built snow forts. Joyfully the boys and girls ran around. They certainly enjoyed the snow.

How	When	Where

Adverbs That Compare

Name _____

Rule Add **-er** to an **adverb** to compare two actions. Add **-est** to compare three or more actions.

Example

*This talent show lasted **longer** than last year's did. It might have lasted **longest** of all the shows.*

Exercise Circle the correct form of each adverb in parentheses.

1. Cheryl sang (softer, softest) of all the performers.

2. Bill danced (slower, slowest) than Philip.

3. Jill played the drums (louder, loudest) of all the drummers.

4. Carlos sang (longer, longest) than Rita.

5. Jenny tap-danced (faster, fastest) than Paul.

6. Kim Tung threw the baton (higher, highest) of all the twirlers.

Rule If an adverb ends with **-ly**, usually add **more** or **most** to make a comparison. Use the word **more** in front of the adverb to compare two actions. Use **most** to compare three or more actions.

Exercise Write **more** or **most** in front of the adverb to make the correct comparison.

1. The audience clapped _____ eagerly this year than last year.

2. Janelle danced _____ daintily of all the ballet dancers.

3. Kristy turned sommersaults _____ smoothly than another girl.

4. Charlie played the violin _____ brilliantly of all.

5. Sam read a poem _____ successfully than Ginger.

6. Shamara danced _____ gracefully than Karen.

Adding Adverbs

Rule Adding **adverbs** to sentences to describe the action makes sentences more interesting and specific.

Example

Danny watched the animals.
*Danny **quietly** watched the animals.* **(how)**
***Yesterday** Danny watched the animals.* **(when)**
*Danny watched the animals **outside**.* **(where)*

Exercise Rewrite each sentence, adding an adverb from the box to make the sentence more interesting and specific. Do not repeat an adverb. You will not use all the adverbs.

outside	slowly	easily	later	higher	sometimes
playfully	down	there	often	sadly	smoothly
regularly	daily	better	simply	best	beautifully

1. My family visited the zoo.

   _____

2. I took pictures.

   _____

3. The peacock opened its feathers.

   _____

4. I liked the polar bears.

   _____

5. The monkeys climbed.

   _____

6. An elephant sprayed water on me.

   _____

7. The giraffe chewed leaves.

   _____

8. A snake crawled.

   _____

Adjective and Adverb Placement in Sentences

Name _____

- An **adjective** may be placed directly before the noun it describes or it may be used after a linking verb to describe the subject.

    *The **beautiful** painting hangs in a museum.* (adjective)
    *The painting is **beautiful**.* (adjective)

- An **adverb** may be used directly after an action verb or it may be placed elsewhere in a sentence.

    *The artist painted **skillfully**.* (adverb)
    ***Skillfully** he made the colors come alive.* (adverb)

Exercise Write **ADJ** above the boldfaced word if it is an adjective. Write **ADV** if it is an adverb.

1. **One** painting showed a **young** girl exercising **gracefully**.

2. A boy gazed **thoughtfully** out an **open** window.

3. A **huge** painting of Monet's hung **nearby**.

4. The **pale** waterlilies filled the canvas **completely**.

5. Renoir painted **simple** scenes of **everyday** life.

6. Picasso painted in **various** styles.

7. His use of **bright** colors and **odd** shapes was **interesting**.

8. Matisse's style of painting changed **gradually** over the years.

9. **First** he imitated **other** artists.

10. **Eventually** Matisse developed a **unique** style.

11. He used **bold** colors **skillfully**.

12. Matisse **always** painted using **interesting color** combinations.

Writing with Adjectives and Adverbs

Name _____

Rule An **adjective** is used to describe a noun. An **adverb** describes a verb.

Example

*We went into the **busy** pet store. (adjective)*
*Dad and I walked **quickly** through the mall. (adverb)*

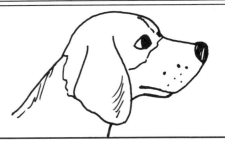

Exercise Read all of the sentences below. Choose an adjective or an adverb to describe each bold-faced word. Write it in the blank. Rewrite each sentence. Do not use any adjective or adverb more than once.

Adjectives		Adverbs	
white	many	immediately	straight
adorable	best	excitedly	pitifully

1. Dad and I **went** _____ to the back wall.

_____

2. We saw _____ animal **cages**.

_____

3. The _____ **puppies** interested me most.

_____

4. One little beagle **wiggled** _____ .

_____

5. I _____ **knew** this was the one I wanted.

_____

6. He was black and brown with _____ **spots**.

_____

7. He **whined** _____ .

_____

8. A puppy would be the _____ **present** I could have.

_____

Contractions

Name _____

Rule A **contraction** is a word made by joining two words with one or more letters left out. An apostrophe is used in the place of any missing letters.

Example

I will – **I'll**   she would – **she'd**
he has – **he's**   they are – **they're**

Exercise Write the contraction for each pair of words.

1. you are _____
2. has not _____
3. we have _____
4. you had _____
5. I had _____
6. she is _____
7. they are _____
8. she has _____
9. should not _____
10. they have _____

11. they will _____
12. does not _____
13. I am _____
14. he is _____
15. will not _____
16. do not _____
17. I have _____
18. you would _____
19. can not _____
20. we are _____

• Rewrite the sentences, replacing the boldfaced words with the correct contraction.

1. I **do not** know if **I will** be able to go tomorrow either.

_____

2. If I **cannot** go, Raul said **he would** go with Rosa.

_____

3. Rosa will be disappointed if she **does not** get to go.

_____

4. The Monet exhibit **will not** be there much longer.

_____

Sentences, Fragments, and Run-ons

Name _____

Rule A **complete sentence** tells a complete thought. It contains a subject and a predicate. A **sentence fragment** does not express a complete thought. A **run-on sentence** is two or more sentences written together without correct punctuation.

Example

Mr. Wilkins went to Alaska last year.
   (complete sentence)
First Mr. Wilkins.
   (sentence fragment)
He flew to Seattle then he took a plane to Anchorage.
   (run-on sentence)

Exercise   Write **C** for complete, **F** for fragment, or **R** for run-on.

_____ 1. Life for children in an Eskimo village is much like life in any town.

_____ 2. The boys and girls.

_____ 3. Children go to school just as you do.

_____ 4. They study reading and English they do math problems and learn to spell and write.

_____ 5. They say the Pledge of Allegiance to the flag before beginning their school work.

_____ 6. Many of the boys and girls wear warm parkas with fur hoods.

_____ 7. They wear warm boots to keep their feet from getting cold.

_____ 8. During festivals, children play games and have contests, they enjoy a game of blanket toss in which the child has to keep his or her balance while being tossed in the air from a blanket of walrus skin.

_____ 9. They also like.

_____ 10. Today, many families have trucks and snowmobiles for transportation rather than dogsleds.

_____ 11. Instead of using kayaks, a small boat.

_____ 12. Some Eskimos use aluminum boats with motors to go fishing.

_____ 13. Some Eskimos still use harpoons to kill seals.

_____ 14. *Muktuk*, the skin and layer of blubber from a black whale.

Answer Key

Grammar
Grade 3

Four Kinds of Sentences
Name _____

Rule Always begin a sentence with a capital letter. End a statement or a command with a period. End a question with a question mark. End an exclamation with an exclamation point.

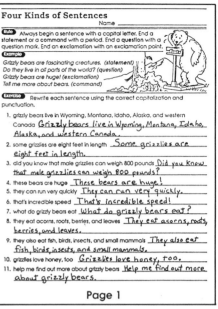

Example
Grizzly bears are fascinating creatures. (statement)
Do they live in all parts of the world? (question)
Grizzly bears are huge! (exclamation)
Tell me more about bears. (command)

Exercise Rewrite each sentence using the correct capitalization and punctuation.

1. grizzly bears live in Wyoming, Montana, Idaho, Alaska, and western Canada *Grizzly bears live in Wyoming, Montana, Idaho, Alaska, and western Canada.*
2. some grizzlies are eight feet in length *Some grizzlies are eight feet in length.*
3. did you know that male grizzlies can weigh 800 pounds *Did you know that male grizzlies can weigh 800 pounds?*
4. these bears are huge *These bears are huge!*
5. they can run very quickly *They can run very quickly.*
6. that's incredible speed *That's incredible speed!*
7. what do grizzly bears eat *What do grizzly bears eat?*
8. they eat acorns, roots, berries, and leaves *They eat acorns, roots, berries, and leaves.*
9. they also eat fish, birds, insects, and small mammals *They also eat fish, birds, insects, and small mammals.*
10. grizzlies love honey, too *Grizzlies love honey, too.*
11. help me find out more about grizzly bears *Help me find out more about grizzly bears.*

Page 1

Statements
Name _____

Rule A statement is a sentence that tells something. It begins with a capital letter and ends with a period.

Mercury is the planet closest to the sun.

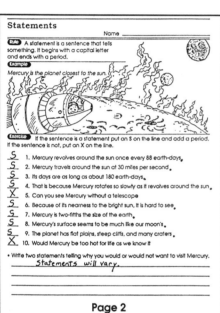

Exercise If the sentence is a statement put an S on the line and add a period. If the sentence is not, put an X on the line.

S 1. Mercury revolves around the sun once every 88 earth-days.
S 2. Mercury travels around the sun at 30 miles per second.
S 3. Its days are as long as about 180 earth-days.
S 4. That is because Mercury rotates so slowly as it revolves around the sun.
X 5. Can you see Mercury without a telescope
S 6. Because of its nearness to the bright sun, it is hard to see.
S 7. Mercury is two-fifths the size of the earth.
S 8. Mercury's surface seems to be much like our moon's.
S 9. The planet has flat plains, steep cliffs, and many craters.
X 10. Would Mercury be too hot for life as we know it

• Write two statements telling why you would or would not want to visit Mercury.
Statements will vary.

Page 2

Questions
Name _____

Rule A question is a sentence that asks something. It begins with a capital letter and ends with a question mark.

Why is Mars known as the red planet?

Exercise If the sentence is a question, add a question mark and color the circle red. If it is not a question, put an X on the circle.

1. How many miles is Mars from the sun?
2. Can you see Mars without a telescope?
3. (X) Mars is the fourth planet from the sun
4. Did you know there are only two planets which are smaller than Mars?
5. Would plants and animals be able to live on Mars?
6. What is the surface temperature on Mars?
7. Does Mars have polar caps like the earth?
8. Are there mountains and volcanoes on the planet?
9. Is much of its surface desertlike?
10. When do you think a manned spacecraft will go to Mars?

• Rewrite each statement as a question by changing the word order.

1. Clouds can be seen on Mars.
Can clouds be seen on Mars?
2. Mars does have two moons.
Does Mars have two moons?
3. The moons are named Phobos and Deimos.
Are the moons named Phobos and Deimos?
4. Space probes have landed on Mars.
Have space probes landed on Mars?

Page 3

Exclamatory and Command Sentences
Name _____

Rule An exclamatory sentence is a sentence that shows strong feeling or surprise. It begins with a capital letter and ends with an exclamation point.

Example
I won a trip around the world!

Rule A command sentence tells someone to do something. A command begins with a capital letter and ends with a period.

Get my suitcase.

Exercise Add the correct punctuation to the end of each sentence. Then color the exclamatory sentences blue and the commands green.

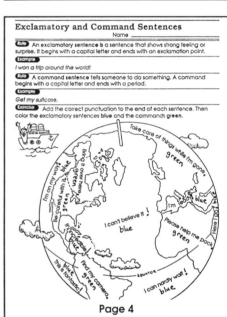

Page 4

Word Order in Sentences
Name _____

Rule You can often make a question out of a statement by changing the word order of the sentence.

Example
My family is going on a camping trip. (statement)
Is my family going on a camping trip? (question)

Exercise Change the word order to make each statement a question and each question a statement. Write the new sentence on the line.

1. Mom and Dad are going to take turns driving.
Are Mom and Dad going to take turns driving?
2. Ellen is getting the gear together.
Is Ellen getting the gear together?
3. James is packing the car trunk.
Is James packing the car trunk?
4. Will it be dark when we arrive at the lake?
It will be dark when we arrive at the lake.
5. Joey's job is to put up the tent.
Is Joey's job to put up the tent?
6. I can help by inflating the air mattresses.
Can I help by inflating the air mattresses?
7. Will we sit around the fire and tell stories?
We will sit around the fire and tell stories.
8. Will I be allowed to roast marshmallows the first night?
I will be allowed to roast marshmallows the first night.
9. Camping is fun for most families.
Is camping fun for most families?

Page 5

Nouns
Name _____

Rule A noun names a person, place, or thing.

A teacher at my school read a book.

Exercise Color each book blue if the word in it is a noun. Put an X on each word which is not a noun.

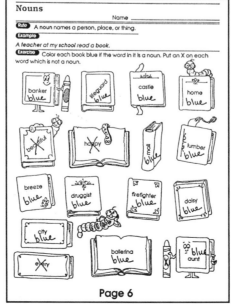

banker — blue
Xwood
castle — blue
home — blue
Xbeautiful
Xhappy
mail — blue
lumber — blue
breeze — blue
Xnoisy
druggist — blue
firefighter — blue
daisy — blue
city — blue
ballerina — blue
Xevery
aunt — blue

Page 6

More Nouns
Name _____

Rule A noun names a person, place, or thing.

Some scientists study plants and animals that live in tropical forests.

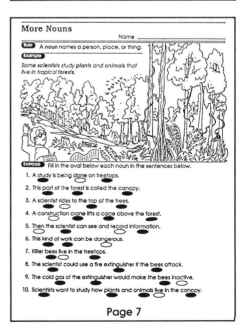

Exercise Fill in the oval below each noun in the sentences below.

1. A study is being done on treetops.
2. This part of the forest is called the canopy.
3. A scientist rides to the top of the trees.
4. A construction crane lifts a cage above the forest.
5. Then the scientist can see and record information.
6. This kind of work can be dangerous.
7. Killer bees live in the treetops.
8. The scientist could use a fire extinguisher if the bees attack.
9. The cold gas of the extinguisher would make the bees inactive.
10. Scientists want to study how plants and animals live in the canopy.

Page 7

Singular and Plural Nouns

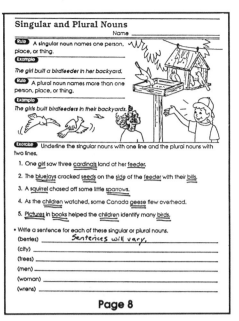

Rule A singular noun names one person, place, or thing.

Example
The girl built a birdfeeder in her backyard.

Rule A plural noun names more than one person, place, or thing.

Example
The girls built birdfeeders in their backyards.

Exercise Underline the singular nouns with one line and the plural nouns with two lines.

1. One girl saw three cardinals land at her feeder.
2. The bluejays cracked seeds on the side of the feeder with their bills.
3. A squirrel chased off some little sparrows.
4. As the children watched, some Canada geese flew overhead.
5. Pictures in books helped the children identify many birds.

• Write a sentence for each of these singular or plural nouns.
(berries) _Sentences will vary._
(city) _____
(trees) _____
(men) _____
(woman) _____
(wrens) _____

Page 8

Plural Nouns

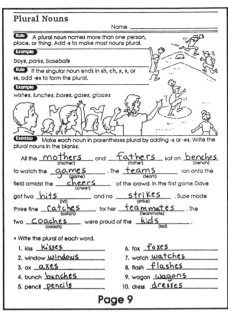

Rule A plural noun names more than one person, place, or thing. Add -s to make most nouns plural.

Example
boys, parks, baseballs

Rule If the singular noun ends in sh, ch, x, s, or ss, add -es to form the plural.

Example
wishes, lunches, boxes, gases, glasses

Exercise Make each noun in parentheses plural by adding -s or -es. Write the plural nouns in the blanks.

All the __mothers__ (mother) and __fathers__ (father) sat on __benches__ (bench) to watch the __games__ (game). The __teams__ (team) ran onto the field amidst the __cheers__ (cheer) of the crowd. In the first game Dave got two __hits__ (hit) and no __strikes__ (strike). Suzie made three fine __catches__ (catch) for her __teammates__ (teammate). The two __coaches__ (coach) were proud of the __kids__ (kid).

• Write the plural of each word.
1. kiss __kisses__   6. fox __foxes__
2. window __windows__   7. watch __watches__
3. ax __axes__   8. flash __flashes__
4. bunch __bunches__   9. wagon __wagons__
5. pencil __pencils__   10. dress __dresses__

Page 9

More Plural Nouns

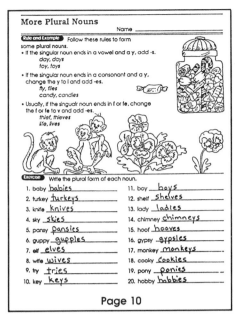

Rule and Example Follow these rules to form some plural nouns.
• If the singular noun ends in a vowel and a y, add -s.
  day, days
  toy, toys
• If the singular noun ends in a consonant and a y, change the y to i and add -es.
  fly, flies
  candy, candies
• Usually, if the singular noun ends in f or fe, change the f or fe to v and add -es.
  thief, thieves
  life, lives

Exercise Write the plural form of each noun.
1. baby __babies__   11. boy __boys__
2. turkey __turkeys__   12. shelf __shelves__
3. knife __knives__   13. lady __ladies__
4. sky __skies__   14. chimney __chimneys__
5. pansy __pansies__   15. hoof __hooves__
6. guppy __guppies__   16. gypsy __gypsies__
7. elf __elves__   17. monkey __monkeys__
8. wife __wives__   18. cooky __cookies__
9. try __tries__   19. pony __ponies__
10. key __keys__   20. hobby __hobbies__

Page 10

Proper Nouns

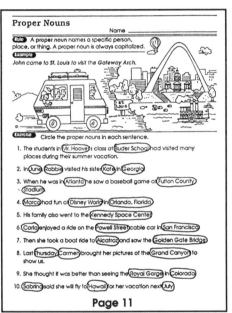

Rule A proper noun names a specific person, place, or thing. A proper noun is always capitalized.

Example
John came to St. Louis to visit the Gateway Arch.

Exercise Circle the proper nouns in each sentence.

1. The students in Mr. Hoover's class at Buder School had visited many places during their summer vacation.
2. In June, Robbie visited his sister Kate in Georgia.
3. When he was in Atlanta he saw a baseball game at Fulton County Stadium.
4. Marco had fun at Disney World in Orlando, Florida.
5. His family also went to the Kennedy Space Center.
6. Carla enjoyed a ride on the Powell Street cable car in San Francisco.
7. Then she took a boat ride to Alcatraz and saw the Golden Gate Bridge.
8. Last Thursday, Carmen brought her pictures of the Grand Canyon to show us.
9. She thought it was better than seeing the Royal Gorge in Colorado.
10. Sabrina said she will fly to Hawaii for her vacation next July.

Page 11

Possessive Nouns

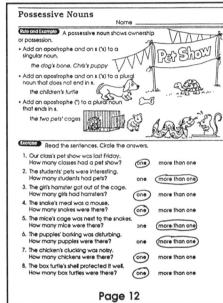

Rule and Example A possessive noun shows ownership or possession.
• Add an apostrophe and an s ('s) to a singular noun.
  the dog's bone, Chris's puppy
• Add an apostrophe and an s ('s) to a plural noun that does not end in s.
  the children's turtle
• Add an apostrophe (') to a plural noun that ends in s.
  the two pets' cages

Exercise Read the sentences. Circle the answers.

1. Our class's pet show was last Friday.
   How many classes had a pet show? **one** more than one
2. The students' pets were interesting.
   How many students had pets? one **more than one**
3. The girl's hamster got out of the cage.
   How many girls had hamsters? **one** more than one
4. The snake's meal was a mouse.
   How many snakes were there? **one** more than one
5. The mice's cage was next to the snakes.
   How many mice were there? one **more than one**
6. The puppies' barking was disturbing.
   How many puppies were there? one **more than one**
7. The chicken's clucking was noisy.
   How many chickens were there? **one** more than one
8. The box turtle's shell protected it well.
   How many box turtles were there? **one** more than one

Page 12

Action Verbs

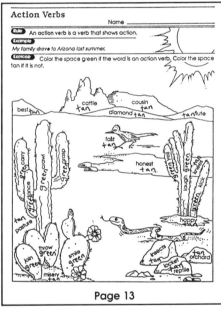

Rule An action verb is a verb that shows action.

Example
My family drove to Arizona last summer.

Example Color the space green if the word is an action verb. Color the space tan if it is not.

Page 13

Present Tense Verbs

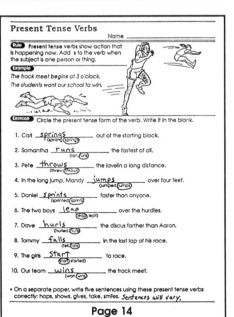

Rule Present tense verbs show action that is happening now. Add -s to the verb when the subject is one person or thing.

Example
The track meet begins at 3 o'clock.
The students want our school to win.

Exercise Circle the present tense form of the verb. Write it in the blank.

1. Carl __springs__ (sprang/springs) out of the starting block.
2. Samantha __runs__ (ran/runs) the fastest of all.
3. Pete __throws__ (threw/throws) the javelin a long distance.
4. In the long jump, Mandy __jumps__ (jumped/jumps) over four feet.
5. Daniel __sprints__ (sprinted/sprints) faster than anyone.
6. The two boys __leap__ (leap/leaped/leapt) over the hurdles.
7. Dave __hurls__ (hurled/hurls) the discus farther than Aaron.
8. Tommy __falls__ (fell/falls) in the last lap of his race.
9. The girls __start__ (start/started) to race.
10. Our team __wins__ (won/wins) the track meet.

• On a separate paper, write five sentences using these present tense verbs correctly: hops, shows, gives, take, smiles. _Sentences will vary._

Page 14

Past Tense Verbs

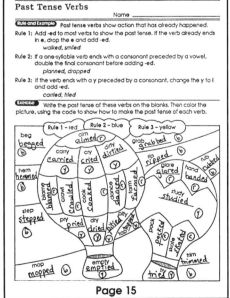

Rule and Example Past tense verbs show action that has already happened.

Rule 1: Add -ed to most verbs to show the past tense. If the verb already ends in e, drop the e and add -ed.
  walked, smiled

Rule 2: If a one-syllable verb ends with a consonant preceded by a vowel, double the final consonant before adding -ed.
  planned, dropped

Rule 3: If the verb ends with a y preceded by a consonant, change the y to i and add -ed.
  carried, fried

Exercise Write the past tense of these verbs on the blanks. Then color the picture, using the code to show how to make the past tense of each verb.

Rule 1 – red   Rule 2 – blue   Rule 3 – yellow

beg begged (b)
aim aimed (r)
carry carried (y)
cry cried (y)
dirty dirtied (r)
grab grabbed (b)
rip ripped (b)
hem hemmed (b)
glare glared (r)
rub rubbed (b)
blame blamed (r)
crawl crawled (r)
dance danced (r)
fan fanned (b)
hand handed (r)
step stepped (b)
pry pried (y)
dry dried (y)
pity pitied (y)
top topped (b)
pack packed (r)
skate skated (r)
mop mopped (b)
empty emptied (y)
trim trimmed (b)
try tried (y)
cook cooked (r)
study studied (y)

Page 15

Helping Verbs

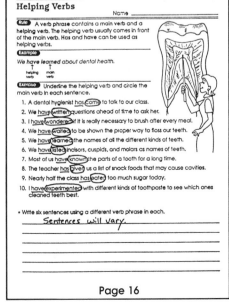

Rule A verb phrase contains a main verb and a helping verb. The helping verb usually comes in front of the main verb. Has and have can be used as helping verbs.

Example
We have learned about dental health.
helping verb / main verb

Exercise Underline the helping verb and circle the main verb in each sentence.

1. A dental hygienist has come to talk to our class.
2. She has written questions ahead of time to ask her.
3. I have wondered if it is really necessary to brush after every meal.
4. We have waited to be shown the proper way to floss our teeth.
5. We have learned the names of all the different kinds of teeth.
6. We have listed incisors, cuspids, and molars as names of teeth.
7. Most of us have known the parts of a tooth for a long time.
8. The teacher has given us a list of snack foods that may cause cavities.
9. Nearly half the class has eaten too much sugar today.
10. I have experimented with different kinds of toothpaste to see which ones cleaned teeth best.

• Write six sentences using a different verb phrase in each.
Sentences will vary.
_____
_____
_____
_____

Page 16

Linking Verbs

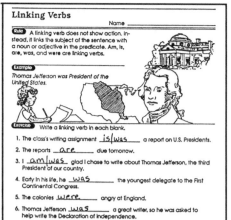

Rule A linking verb does not show action. Instead, it links the subject of the sentence with a noun or adjective in the predicate. Am, is, are, was, and were are linking verbs.

Example
Thomas Jefferson was President of the United States.

Exercise Write a linking verb in each blank.

1. The class's writing assignment **is/was** a report on U.S. Presidents.
2. The reports **are** due tomorrow.
3. I **am/was** glad I chose to write about Thomas Jefferson, the third President of our country.
4. Early in his life, he **was** the youngest delegate to the First Continental Congress.
5. The colonies **were** angry at England.
6. Thomas Jefferson **was** a great writer, so he was asked to help write the Declaration of Independence.
7. The signing of that document **was** an historical event.
8. Later, as President, Jefferson **was** responsible for the Louisiana Purchase.
9. He **was** the first President to live in the White House.
10. Americans **are** fortunate today for the part played in our country's history by Thomas Jefferson.

Page 17

Future Tense Verbs

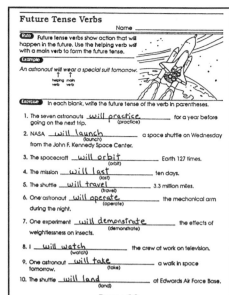

Rule Future tense verbs show action that will happen in the future. Use the helping verb will with a main verb to form the future tense.

Example
An astronaut will wear a special suit tomorrow.
(helping verb) (main verb)

Exercise In each blank, write the future tense of the verb in parentheses.

1. The seven astronauts **will practice** for a year before going on the next trip. (practice)
2. NASA **will launch** a space shuttle on Wednesday from the John F. Kennedy Space Center. (launch)
3. The spacecraft **will orbit** Earth 127 times. (orbit)
4. The mission **will last** ten days. (last)
5. The shuttle **will travel** 3.3 million miles. (travel)
6. One astronaut **will operate** the mechanical arm during the night. (operate)
7. One experiment **will demonstrate** the effects of weightlessness on insects. (demonstrate)
8. I **will watch** the crew at work on television. (watch)
9. One astronaut **will take** a walk in space tomorrow. (take)
10. The shuttle **will land** at Edwards Air Force Base. (land)

Page 18

Irregular Verbs

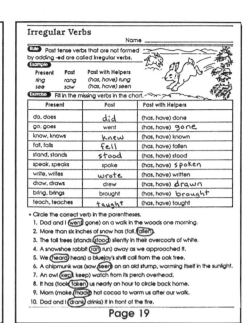

Rule Past tense verbs that are not formed by adding -ed are called irregular verbs.

Example

Present	Past	Past with Helpers
ring	rang	(has, have) rung
see	saw	(has, have) seen

Exercise Fill in the missing verbs in the chart.

Present	Past	Past with Helpers
do, does	**did**	(has, have) done
go, goes	went	(has, have) **gone**
know, knows	**knew**	(has, have) known
fall, falls	**fell**	(has, have) fallen
stand, stands	**stood**	(has, have) stood
speak, speaks	spoke	(has, have) **spoken**
write, writes	**wrote**	(has, have) written
draw, draws	drew	(has, have) **drawn**
bring, brings	brought	(has, have) **brought**
teach, teaches	**taught**	(has, have) taught

• Circle the correct verb in the parentheses.
1. Dad and I (**went**, gone) on a walk in the woods one morning.
2. More than six inches of snow has (fall, (**fallen**)).
3. The tall trees (stands, (**stood**)) silently in their overcoats of white.
4. A snowshoe rabbit ((**ran**), run) away as we approached it.
5. We ((**heard**), hears) a bluejay's shrill call from the oak tree.
6. A chipmunk was (saw, (**seen**)) on an old stump, warming itself in the sunlight.
7. An owl ((**kept**), keep) watch from its perch overhead.
8. It has (took, (**taken**)) us nearly an hour to circle back home.
9. Mom (make, (**made**)) hot cocoa to warm us after our walk.
10. Dad and I (**drank**), drinks) it in front of the fire.

Page 19

More Irregular Verbs

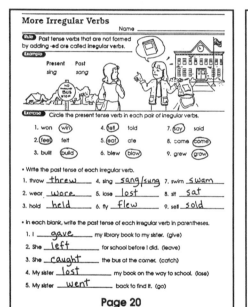

Rule Past tense verbs that are not formed by adding -ed are called irregular verbs.

Example

Present	Past
sing	sang

Exercise Circle the present tense verb in each pair of irregular verbs.

1. won (**win**)   4. (**fell**) told   7. (**say**) said
2. (**feel**) felt   5. (**eat**) ate   8. came (**come**)
3. built (**build**)   6. blew (**blow**)   9. grew (**grow**)

• Write the past tense of each irregular verb.
1. throw **threw**   4. sing **sang/sung**   7. swim **swam**
2. wear **wore**   5. lose **lost**   8. sit **sat**
3. hold **held**   6. fly **flew**   9. sell **sold**

• In each blank, write the past tense of each irregular verb in parentheses.
1. I **gave** my library book to my sister. (give)
2. She **left** for school before I did. (leave)
3. She **caught** the bus at the corner. (catch)
4. My sister **lost** my book on the way to school. (lose)
5. My sister **went** back to find it. (go)

Page 20

Subjects of Sentences

Rule The subject of a sentence tells whom or what the sentence is about.

Example
The buffalo provided the Plains Indians with many things.
(subject)

Exercise Underline the subject of each sentence.

1. The Plains Indians used almost every part of the buffalo.
2. Their tepees were made of buffalo hides.
3. Clothing was made from the hides of buffalo and deer.
4. Plains Indians ate the meat of the buffalo.
5. Buffalo stomachs were used as pots for cooking.
6. Bones were used for tools and utensils.
7. The tail was used as a fly swatter.
8. Horns were used as scrapers and cups.
9. The buffalo manure was dried and used for fuel.
10. A kind of glue could be made from the hooves.

• If the word group could be the subject of a sentence, put a check mark (✔) on the line. If it could not be the subject of a sentence, put an X.

✔ 1. feathers, beads, and paint   ✘ 4. wore moccasins
✔ 2. the headdress   ✔ 5. bear claw necklaces
✘ 3. decorated their clothes   ✔ 6. the chief

Page 21

Simple and Complete Subjects

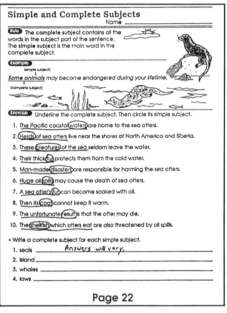

Rule The complete subject contains all the words in the subject part of the sentence. The simple subject is the main word in the complete subject.

Example
(simple subject)
Some animals may become endangered during your lifetime.
(complete subject)

Exercise Underline the complete subject. Then circle its simple subject.

1. The Pacific coastal **waters** are home to the sea otters.
2. **Herds** of sea otters live near the shores of North America and Siberia.
3. These **creatures** of the sea seldom leave the water.
4. Their thick **fur** protects them from the cold water.
5. Man-made **disasters** are responsible for harming the sea otters.
6. Huge oil **spills** may cause the death of sea otters.
7. A sea otter's **fur** can become soaked with oil.
8. Then its **coat** cannot keep it warm.
9. The unfortunate **result** is that the otter may die.
10. The **shellfish**, which otters eat, are also threatened by oil spills.

• Write a complete subject for each simple subject.
1. seals **Answers will vary.**
2. island ___
3. whales ___
4. laws ___

Page 22

Compound Subjects

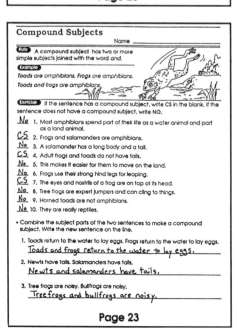

Rule A compound subject has two or more simple subjects joined with the word and.

Example
Toads are amphibians. Frogs are amphibians.
Toads and frogs are amphibians.

Exercise If the sentence has a compound subject, write CS in the blank. If the sentence does not have a compound subject, write NO.

No 1. Most amphibians spend part of their life as a water animal and part as a land animal.
CS 2. Frogs and salamanders are amphibians.
No 3. A salamander has a long body and a tail.
CS 4. Adult frogs and toads do not have tails.
No 5. This makes it easier for them to move on the land.
No 6. Frogs use their strong hind legs for leaping.
CS 7. The eyes and nostrils of a frog are on top of its head.
No 8. Tree frogs are expert jumpers and can cling to things.
No 9. Horned toads are not amphibians.
No 10. They are really reptiles.

• Combine the subject parts of the two sentences to make a compound subject. Write the new sentence on the line.
1. Toads return to the water to lay eggs. Frogs return to the water to lay eggs.
Toads and frogs return to the water to lay eggs.
2. Newts have tails. Salamanders have tails.
Newts and salamanders have tails.
3. Tree frogs are noisy. Bullfrogs are noisy.
Tree frogs and bullfrogs are noisy.

Page 23

Predicates of Sentences

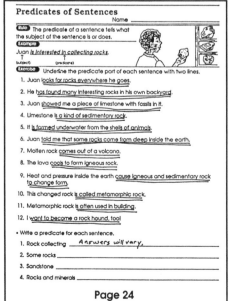

Rule The predicate of a sentence tells what the subject of the sentence is or does.

Example
Juan is interested in collecting rocks.
(subject) (predicate)

Exercise Underline the predicate part of each sentence with two lines.

1. Juan looks for rocks everywhere he goes.
2. He has found many interesting rocks in his own backyard.
3. Juan showed me a piece of limestone with fossils in it.
4. Limestone is a kind of sedimentary rock.
5. It is formed underwater from the shells of animals.
6. Juan told me that some rocks come from deep inside the earth.
7. Molten rock comes out of a volcano.
8. The lava cools to form igneous rock.
9. Heat and pressure inside the earth cause igneous and sedimentary rock to change form.
10. This changed rock is called metamorphic rock.
11. Metamorphic rock is often used in building.
12. I want to become a rock hound, too!

• Write a predicate for each sentence.
1. Rock collecting **Answers will vary.**
2. Some rocks ___
3. Sandstone ___
4. Rocks and minerals ___

Page 24

Simple and Complete Predicates

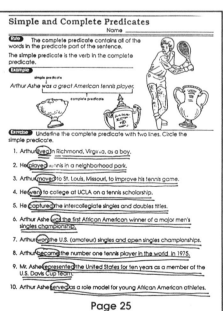

Rule The complete predicate contains all of the words in the predicate part of the sentence. The simple predicate is the verb in the complete predicate.

Example
simple predicate
Arthur Ashe was a great American tennis player.
complete predicate

Exercise Underline the complete predicate with two lines. Circle the simple predicate.

1. Arthur **lived** in Richmond, Virginia, as a boy.
2. He **played** tennis in a neighborhood park.
3. Arthur **moved** to St. Louis, Missouri, to improve his tennis game.
4. He **went** to college at UCLA on a tennis scholarship.
5. He **captured** the intercollegiate singles and doubles titles.
6. Arthur Ashe **was** the first African American winner of a major men's singles championship.
7. Arthur **won** the U.S. (amateur) singles and open singles championships.
8. He **became** the number one tennis player in the world in 1975.
9. Mr. Ashe **represented** the United States for ten years as a member of the U.S. Davis Cup Team.
10. Arthur Ashe **served** as a role model for young African American athletes.

Page 25

IF5075 Grammar

Compound Predicates

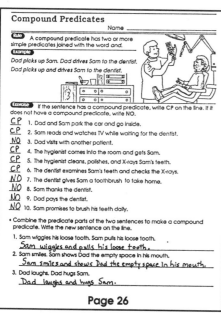

Rule A compound predicate has two or more simple predicates joined with the word *and*.

Dad picks up Sam. Dad drives Sam to the dentist.
Dad picks up and drives Sam to the dentist.

Exercise If the sentence has a compound predicate, write CP on the line. If it does not have a compound predicate, write NO.

CP 1. Dad and Sam park the car and go inside.
CP 2. Sam reads and watches TV while waiting for the dentist.
NO 3. Dad visits with another patient.
CP 4. The hygienist comes into the room and gets Sam.
CP 5. The hygienist cleans, polishes, and X-rays Sam's teeth.
CP 6. The dentist examines Sam's teeth and checks the X-rays.
NO 7. The dentist gives Sam a toothbrush to take home.
NO 8. Sam thanks the dentist.
NO 9. Dad pays the dentist.
NO 10. Sam promises to brush his teeth daily.

• Combine the predicate parts of the two sentences to make a compound predicate. Write the new sentence on the line.

1. Sam wiggles his loose tooth. Sam pulls his loose tooth.
   Sam wiggles and pulls his loose tooth.
2. Sam smiles. Sam shows Dad the empty space in his mouth.
   Sam smiles and shows Dad the empty space in his mouth.
3. Dad laughs. Dad hugs Sam.
   Dad laughs and hugs Sam.

Page 26

Compound Sentences

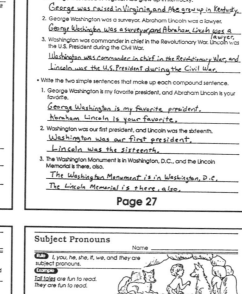

Rule Use a comma and the word *and* to connect two simple sentences to make a compound sentence.

George Washington was born in 1732, and Abraham Lincoln was born in 1809.

Exercise Combine the two sentences to make a compound sentence.

1. George was raised in Virginia. Abe grew up in Kentucky.
   George was raised in Virginia, and Abe grew up in Kentucky.
2. George Washington was a surveyor. Abraham Lincoln was a lawyer.
   George Washington was a surveyor, and Abraham Lincoln was a lawyer.
3. Washington was commander in chief in the Revolutionary War. Lincoln was the U.S. President during the Civil War.
   Washington was commander in chief in the Revolutionary War, and Lincoln was the U.S. President during the Civil War.

• Write the two simple sentences that make up each compound sentence.

1. George Washington is my favorite president, and Abraham Lincoln is your favorite.
   George Washington is my favorite president.
   Abraham Lincoln is your favorite.
2. Washington was our first president, and Lincoln was the sixteenth.
   Washington was our first president.
   Lincoln was the sixteenth.
3. The Washington Monument is in Washington, D.C., and the Lincoln Memorial is there, also.
   The Washington Monument is in Washington, D.C.
   The Lincoln Memorial is there, also.

Page 27

Subject-Verb Agreement

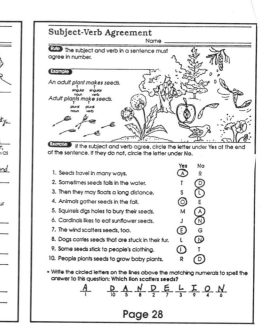

Rule The subject and verb in a sentence must agree in number.

An adult plant makes seeds.
Adult plants make seeds.

Exercise If the subject and verb agree, circle the letter under Yes at the end of the sentence. If they do not, circle the letter under No.

	Yes	No
1. Seeds travel in many ways.	(A)	R
2. Sometimes seeds falls in the water.	T	(D)
3. Then they may floats a long distance.	S	(L)
4. Animals gather seeds in the fall.	(O)	E
5. Squirrels digs holes to bury their seeds.	M	(A)
6. Cardinals likes to eat sunflower seeds.	J	(N)
7. The wind scatters seeds, too.	(E)	G
8. Dogs carries seeds that are stuck in their fur.	L	(N)
9. Some seeds stick to people's clothing.	(I)	T
10. People plants seeds to grow baby plants.	R	(D)

• Write the circled letters on the lines above the matching numerals to spell the answer to this question: Which lion scatters seeds?

A D A N D E L I O N
1 10 5 8 2 7 3 9 4 6

Page 28

Possessive Pronouns

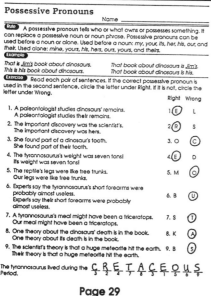

Rule A possessive pronoun tells who or what owns or possesses something. It can replace a possessive noun or noun phrase. Possessive pronouns can be used before a noun or alone. Used before a noun: *my, your, its, her, his, our,* and *their.* Used alone: *mine, yours, his, hers, ours, yours,* and *theirs.*

That is Jim's book about dinosaurs.   *That book about dinosaurs is Jim's.*
This is his book about dinosaurs.   *That book about dinosaurs is his.*

Exercise Read each pair of sentences. If the correct possessive pronoun is used in the second sentence, circle the letter under Right. If it is not, circle the letter under Wrong.

	Right	Wrong
1. A paleontologist studies dinosaurs' remains. A paleontologist studies their remains.	(E)	L
2. The important discovery was the scientist's. The important discovery was hers.	(R)	S
3. She found part of a dinosaur's tooth. She found part of their tooth.	O	(C)
4. The tyrannosaurus's weight was seven tons! Its weight was seven tons!	(E)	D
5. The reptile's legs were like tree trunks. Our legs were like tree trunks.	M	(C)
6. Experts say the tyrannosaurus's short forearms were probably almost useless. Experts say their short forearms were probably almost useless.	B	(U)
7. A tyrannosaurus's meal might have been a triceratops. Our meal might have been a triceratops.	S	(T)
8. One theory about the dinosaurs' death is in the book. One theory about its death is in the book.	K	(A)
9. The scientist's theory is that a huge meteorite hit the earth. Their theory is that a huge meteorite hit the earth.	B	(S)

The tyrannosaurus lived during the C R E T A C E O U S Period.
                                    3 2 4 7 8 3 5 6 6 9

Page 29

Subject Pronouns

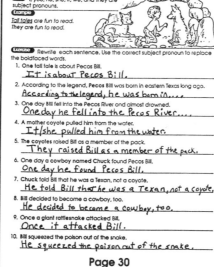

Rule *I, you, he, she, it, we,* and *they* are subject pronouns.

Tall tales are fun to read.
They are fun to read.

Exercise Rewrite each sentence. Use the correct subject pronoun to replace the boldfaced words.

1. One tall tale is about Pecos Bill.
   It is about Pecos Bill.
2. According to the legend, Pecos Bill was born in eastern Texas long ago.
   According to the legend, he was born in....
3. One day Bill fell into the Pecos River and almost drowned.
   One day he fell into the Pecos River....
4. A mother coyote pulled him from the water.
   It/she pulled him from the water.
5. The coyotes raised Bill as a member of the pack.
   They raised Bill as a member of the pack.
6. One day a cowboy named Chuck found Pecos Bill.
   One day he found Pecos Bill.
7. Chuck told Bill that he was a Texan, not a coyote.
   He told Bill that he was a Texan, not a coyote.
8. Bill decided to become a cowboy, too.
   He decided to become a cowboy, too.
9. Once a giant rattlesnake attacked Bill.
   Once it attacked Bill.
10. Bill squeezed the poison out of the snake.
    He squeezed the poison out of the snake.

Page 30

Object Pronouns

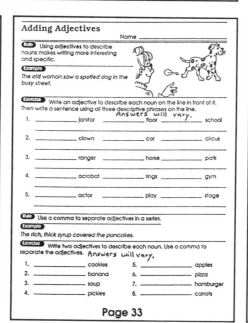

Rule Object pronouns are pronouns which come after action verbs in a sentence. *Me, you, him, her, it, us,* and *them* are object pronouns.

Pecos Bill wrestled a gigantic monster.
Pecos Bill wrestled it.

Exercise Rewrite each sentence. Replace the words in boldfaced type with the correct object pronoun.

1. Pecos Bill invented cattle roping and branding.
   Pecos Bill invented them.
2. He scared a steer out of its skin with a coyote howl.
   He scared it out of its skin with a coyote howl.
3. Bill used the hide to make lassos for all the cowboys.
   Bill used it to make lassos for all the cowboys.
4. Bill wanted a horse to ride on a roundup.
   Bill wanted it to ride on a roundup.
5. Bill captured a wild stallion called Lightning.
   Bill captured it.
6. The horse crossed three states trying to buck Bill.
   The horse crossed three states trying to buck Bill.
7. Bill calmed the horse by singing in coyote language.
   Bill calmed it by singing in coyote language.
8. Then Bill met Slewfoot Sue and fell in love.
   The Bill met her and fell in love.
9. Unfortunately, Lightning bucked Slewfoot Sue up to the moon.
   Unfortunately, Lightning bucked her up to the moon.
10. Bill lassoed a tornado to help him save Sue.
    Bill lassoed it to help him save Sue.

Page 31

Adjectives

Rule An adjective is a word that describes a noun or pronoun. Adjectives answer the questions how many, what kind, or which one.

Two students brought colorful insects to class.
 (how many)   (what kind)

Exercise Circle the adjective that describes each underlined noun.

1. Many scorpions live in the desert.
2. Scorpions have a poisonous sting.
3. A sting can kill a small child.
4. Scorpions hide in dark places during the day.
5. They crawl under rotten logs and beneath rocks.
6. Giant scorpions can be five inches long.
7. Scorpions eat desert insects.
8. They can go without water for one year.
9. Rattlesnakes also live on the southwestern deserts.
10. They are poisonous snakes.
11. The poison comes out of two fangs.
12. The small horned rattler is also called a sidewinder.
13. Rattlesnakes eat small mammals and birds.

Page 32

Adding Adjectives

Rule Using adjectives to describe nouns makes writing more interesting and specific.

The old woman saw a spotted dog in the busy street.

Exercise Write an adjective to describe each noun on the line in front of it. Then write a sentence using all three descriptive phrases on the line.

Answers will vary.

1.	_____ janitor	_____ floor	_____ school
2.	_____ clown	_____ car	_____ circus
3.	_____ ranger	_____ horse	_____ park
4.	_____ acrobat	_____ rings	_____ gym
5.	_____ actor	_____ play	_____ stage

Rule Use a comma to separate adjectives in a series.

The rich, thick syrup covered the pancakes.

Exercise Write two adjectives to describe each noun. Use a comma to separate the adjectives. Answers will vary.

1. _____ cookies	5. _____ apples
2. _____ banana	6. _____ pizza
3. _____ soup	7. _____ hamburger
4. _____ pickles	8. _____ carrots

Page 33

Adjectives That Compare

Rule Add *-er* to most adjectives when comparing two nouns. Add *-est* to most adjectives when comparing three or more nouns.

The forecaster said this winter is colder than last winter.
It is the coldest winter on record.

Exercise Write the correct form of the adjective in parentheses.

1. The weather map showed that the **coldest** (cold) place of all was Fargo, North Dakota.
2. The **warmest** (warm) city of all was Needles, California.
3. Does San Diego get **hotter** (hot) than San Francisco?
4. The **deepest** (deep) snow of all fell in Buffalo, New York.
5. That snowfall was two inches **deeper** (deep) than in Syracuse.
6. The **windiest** (windy) place of all was Wichita, Kansas.
7. The **strongest** (strong) winds of all blew there.
8. The **foggiest** (foggy) city in the U.S. was Chicago.
9. Seattle was the **rainiest** (rainy) of all the cities listed on the map.
10. It is usually **rainier** (rainy) in Seattle than in Portland.
11. I just hope tomorrow is **sunnier** (sunny) than it was today.
12. Today has been the **cloudiest** (cloudy) day all week.

Page 34

IF5075 Grammar

Proper Adjectives

Name _____

Rule A proper adjective is a word that describes a noun or a pronoun. A proper adjective always begins with a capital letter.

Example
The American flag waves proudly over the United States capitol.

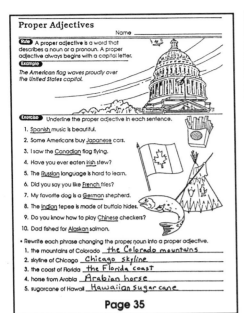

Exercise Underline the proper adjective in each sentence.
1. Spanish music is beautiful.
2. Some Americans buy Japanese cars.
3. I saw the Canadian flag flying.
4. Have you ever eaten Irish stew?
5. The Russian language is hard to learn.
6. Did you say you like French fries?
7. My favorite dog is a German shepherd.
8. The Indian tepee is made of buffalo hides.
9. Do you know how to play Chinese checkers?
10. Dad fished for Alaskan salmon.

• Rewrite each phrase changing the proper noun into a proper adjective.
1. the mountains of Colorado the Colorado mountains
2. skyline of Chicago Chicago skyline
3. the coast of Florida the Florida coast
4. horse from Arabia Arabian horse
5. sugarcane of Hawaii Hawaiian sugar cane

Page 35

Articles

Name _____

Rule and Example A, an, and the are special adjectives called articles.
• Use a before singular nouns beginning with a consonant sound.
  a turtle
• Use an before singular nouns beginning with a vowel sound or a silent h.
  an elephant
• The may be used before singular or plural nouns.
  the parrot   the alligators

Exercise Circle the article which could be used before each noun.
Hint: Sometimes there is more than one answer.

1. camels — a an (the)   16. octopus — a (an) (the)
2. cheetah — (a) an (the)   17. chimpanzee — (a) an (the)
3. gorillas — a an (the)   18. sharks — a an (the)
4. aardvark — a (an) (the)   19. opossum — a (an) (the)
5. eagle — a (an) (the)   20. lion — (a) an (the)
6. jaguars — a an (the)   21. pig — (a) an (the)
7. baboon — (a) an (the)   22. owl — a (an) (the)
8. egret — a (an) (the)   23. dog — (a) an (the)
9. ibex — a (an) (the)   24. pony — (a) an (the)
10. kangaroos — a an (the)   25. whales — a an (the)
11. bird — (a) an (the)   26. dolphin — (a) an (the)
12. tigers — a an (the)   27. ostrich — a (an) (the)
13. ocelot — a (an) (the)   28. rhinoceros — (a) an (the)
14. buffalo — (a) an (the)   29. ox — a (an) (the)
15. hyenas — a an (the)   30. otter — (a) an (the)

Page 36

Adverbs

Name _____

Rule An adverb is a word that can describe a verb. It tells how, when, or where an action takes place.

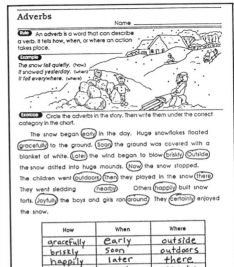

Example
The snow fell quietly. (how)
It snowed yesterday. (when)
It fell everywhere. (where)

Exercise Circle the adverbs in the story. Then write them under the correct category in the chart.

The snow began (early) in the day. Huge snowflakes floated (gracefully) to the ground. (Soon) the ground was covered with a blanket of white. (Later) the wind began to blow (briskly) (Outside) the snow drifted into huge mounds. (Now) the snow stopped. The children went (outdoors) (Then) they played in the snow (there) They went sledding (nearby) Others (happily) built snow forts. (Joyfully) the boys and girls ran (around) They (certainly) enjoyed the snow.

How	When	Where
gracefully	early	outside
briskly	soon	outdoors
happily	later	there
joyfully	now	nearby
certainly	then	around

Page 37

Adverbs That Compare

Name _____

Rule Add -er to an adverb to compare two actions. Add -est to compare three or more actions.

Example
This talent show lasted longer than last year's did. It might have lasted longest of all the shows.

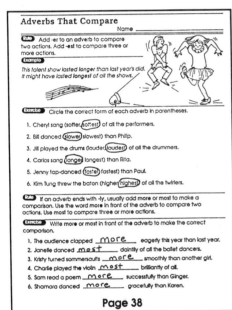

Exercise Circle the correct form of each adverb in parentheses.
1. Cheryl sang (softer, softest) of all the performers.
2. Bill danced (slower) slowest) than Philip.
3. Jill played the drums (louder (loudest) of all the drummers.
4. Carlos sang (longer) longest) than Rita.
5. Jenny tap-danced (faster) fastest) than Paul.
6. Kim Tung threw the baton (higher (highest) of all the twirlers.

Rule If an adverb ends with -ly, usually add more or most to make a comparison. Use the word more in front of the adverb to compare two actions. Use most to compare three or more actions.

Exercise Write more or most in front of the adverb to make the correct comparison.
1. The audience clapped more eagerly this year than last year.
2. Janette danced most daintily of all the ballet dancers.
3. Kristy turned sommersaults more smoothly than any other girl.
4. Charlie played the violin most brilliantly of all.
5. Sam read a poem more successfully than Ginger.
6. Shamara danced more gracefully than Karen.

Page 38

Adding Adverbs

Name _____

Rule Adding adverbs to sentences to describe the action makes sentences more interesting and specific.

Example
Danny watched the animals.
Danny quietly watched the animals. (how)
Yesterday Danny watched the animals. (when)
Danny watched the animals outside. (where)

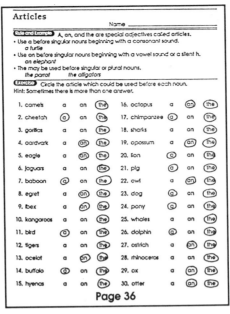

Exercise Rewrite each sentence, adding an adverb from the box to make the sentence more interesting and specific. Do not repeat an adverb. You will not use all the adverbs.

outside	slowly	easily	later	higher	sometimes
playfully	down	there	often	sadly	smoothly
regularly	daily	better	simply	best	beautifully

1. My family visited the zoo.   Answers will vary.
2. I took pictures.
3. The peacock opened its feathers.
4. I liked the polar bears.
5. The monkeys climbed.
6. An elephant sprayed water on me.
7. The giraffe chewed leaves.
8. A snake crawled.

Page 39

Adjective and Adverb Placement in Sentences

Name _____

Rule and Example
• An adjective may be placed directly before the noun it describes or it may be used after a linking verb to describe the subject.
  The beautiful painting hangs in a museum. (adjective)
  The painting is beautiful. (adjective)
• An adverb may be used directly after an action verb or it may be placed elsewhere in a sentence.
  The artist painted skillfully. (adverb)
  Skillfully he made the colors come alive. (adverb)

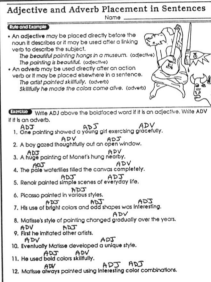

Exercise Write ADJ above the boldfaced word if it is an adjective. Write ADV if it is an adverb.
1. One painting showed a young(ADJ) girl exercising gracefully(ADV).
2. A boy gazed thoughtfully(ADV) out an open(ADJ) window.
3. A huge painting of Monet's hung nearby(ADV).
4. The pale(ADJ) waterlilies filled the canvas completely(ADV).
5. Renoir painted simple(ADJ) scenes of everyday(ADJ) life.
6. Picasso painted in various(ADJ) styles.
7. His use of bright(ADJ) colors and odd(ADJ) shapes was interesting(ADJ).
8. Matisse's style of painting changed gradually(ADV) over the years.
9. First he imitated(ADV) other artists.
10. Eventually(ADV) Matisse developed a unique(ADJ) style.
11. He used bold(ADJ) colors skillfully(ADV).
12. Matisse always(ADV) painted using interesting(ADJ) color(ADJ) combinations.

Page 40

Writing with Adjectives and Adverbs

Name _____

Rule An adjective is used to describe a noun. An adverb describes a verb.

Example
We went into the busy pet store. (adjective)
Dad and I walked quickly through the mall. (adverb)

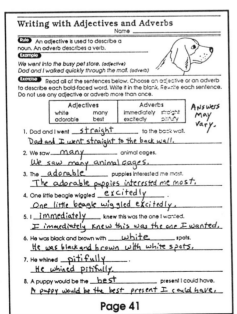

Exercise Read all of the sentences below. Choose an adjective or an adverb to describe the bold-faced word. Write it in the blank. Rewrite each sentence. Do not use any adjective or adverb more than once.

Adjectives		Adverbs	
white	many	immediately	straight
adorable	best	excitedly	pitifully

Answers may vary.

1. Dad and I went straight to the back wall.
   Dad and I went straight to the back wall.
2. We saw many animal cages.
   We saw many animal cages.
3. The adorable puppies interested me most.
   The adorable puppies interested me most.
4. One little beagle wiggled excitedly.
   One little beagle wiggled excitedly.
5. I immediately knew this was the one I wanted.
   I immediately knew this was the one I wanted.
6. He was black and brown with white spots.
   He was black and brown with white spots.
7. He whined pitifully.
   He whined pitifully.
8. A puppy would be the best present I could have.
   A puppy would be the best present I could have.

Page 41

Contractions

Name _____

Rule A contraction is a word made by joining two words with one or more letters left out. An apostrophe is used in the place of any missing letters.

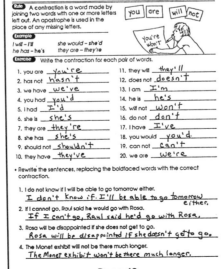

Example
I will – I'll   she would – she'd
he has – he's   they are – they're

Exercise Write the contraction for each pair of words.
1. you are You're   11. they will they'll
2. has not hasn't   12. does not doesn't
3. we have we've   13. I am I'm
4. you had you'd   14. he is he's
5. I had I'd   15. will not won't
6. she is she's   16. do not don't
7. they are they're   17. I have I've
8. she has she's   18. you would you'd
9. should not shouldn't 19. can not can't
10. they have they've   20. we are we're

• Rewrite the sentences, replacing the boldfaced words with the correct contraction.
1. I do not know if I will be able to go tomorrow either.
   I don't know if I'll be able to go tomorrow either.
2. If I cannot go, Raul said he would go with Rosa.
   If I can't go, Raul said he'd go with Rosa.
3. Rosa will be disappointed if she does not get to go.
   Rosa will be disappointed if she doesn't get to go.
4. The Monet exhibit will not be there much longer.
   The Monet exhibit won't be there much longer.

Page 42

Sentences, Fragments, and Run-ons

Name _____

Rule A complete sentence tells a complete thought. It contains a subject and a predicate. A sentence fragment does not express a complete thought. A run-on sentence is two or more sentences written together without correct punctuation.

Example
Mr. Wilkins went to Alaska last year.
(complete sentence)
First Mr. Wilkins.
(sentence fragment)
He flew to Seattle then he took a plane to Anchorage.
(run-on sentence)

Exercise Write C for complete, F for fragment, or R for run-on.
C 1. Life for children in an Eskimo village is much like life in any town.
F 2. The boys and girls.
C 3. Children go to school just as you do.
R 4. They study reading and English they do math problems and learn to spell and write.
C 5. They say the Pledge of Allegiance to the flag before beginning their school work.
C 6. Many of the boys and girls wear warm parkas with fur hoods.
C 7. They wear warm boots to keep their feet from getting cold.
R 8. During festivals, children play games and have contests, they enjoy a game of blanket toss in which the child has to keep his or her balance while being tossed in the air from a blanket of walrus skin.
F 9. They also like.
C 10. Today, many families have trucks and snowmobiles for transportation rather than dogsleds.
F 11. Instead of using kayaks, a small boat.
C 12. Some Eskimos use aluminum boats with motors to go fishing.
C 13. Some Eskimos still use harpoons to kill seals.
F 14. Muktuk, the skin and layer of blubber from a black whale.

Page 43

IF5075 Grammar